DO OPEN

HOW A SIMPLE NEWSLETTER
CAN TRANSFORM YOUR BUSINESS
(AND IT CAN)

DAVID HIEATT

To crazy Mave (my mum)

Published by
The Do Book Company 2017
Works in Progress Publishing Ltd
thedobook.co

Text © David Hieatt 2017
Photography © Andrew Paynter
Photography © Hiut Denim Co
Photography p6 © Dan Rubin
Photography p30, 72 © Jim Marsden
Photography p44, 48, 142 © Marcus Ginns
Illustrations © Tom Fishburne 2017

To find out more about our company,
books and authors, please visit
thedobook.co or follow us **@dobookco**

5% of our proceeds from the
sale of this book is given to
The Do Lectures to help it achieve
its aim of making positive change
thedolectures.com

Cover designed by James Victore
Book designed and set by Ratiotype

Printed and bound by OZGraf Print
on Munken, an FSC-certified paper

MIX
Paper from
responsible sources
FSC® C163799

A CIP catalogue record for this book
is available from the British Library

ISBN 978-1-907974-30-4

10 9 8 7 6 5 4

CONTENTS

DON'T UNDERESTIMATE THEM

I am fascinated by the power of a simple email newsletter to grow a business. I am also fascinated by the fact that most businesses don't pay much attention to theirs. It's an afterthought. A poor cousin. 'Give it to the intern.' And yet, newsletters are one of the most cost-effective ways of talking to your customer that a business can ever have.

But only when they're done right. With skill, with a strategy, with a methodology, they become one of the most effective instruments in your digital toolbox. They build community. They build your brand. And they relentlessly build long-term growth.

I have seen how a simple newsletter built my business, and so I have no doubt it can build yours. Like anything, it requires effort and some smart thinking, but if you take the time and make a commitment, it will help to transform your business. And, it can.

Opposite Me and my wife Clare

NEWSLETTERS ARE NO LONGER IMPORTANT. THEY ARE VITAL

In terms of using social media to grow your business, we are all looking for the next new platform or app. We want to find that magic 'Multiplier' that gets our story out to the world. But there is a danger that, by doing just that, we are ignoring a tried and trusted tool that, well, just works.

Think about it this way. An app can suddenly close overnight. A platform can come and go. And all those millions of followers you have amassed go with it too.

But email isn't going anywhere.

DON'T GIVE IT TO THE INTERN

Newsletters are mostly treated with a lack of respect in big companies. It's not the latest app, it's not the latest platform. It doesn't get written about in the press very often. In short, it is not sexy.

And because of that, people don't treat them with the respect they deserve. They have never tried to do them well, just with the least amount of effort. The newsletter is given to a department that doesn't really want to do it. It is given to the intern who, as smart as they are to impress, may well see the newsletter on a par with making everyone a coffee.

But if you understood its power, you would hand this project to the best people in your business.

MY BACKSTORY
THE DAY I BEGAN TO TAKE NEWSLETTERS SERIOUSLY. LIKE, REALLY SERIOUSLY.

My town used to make jeans. It made 35,000 pairs a week for nearly 40 years. It had Britain's biggest jeans factory. But in 2001, 400 world-class makers lost their jobs. And a town on the far western edge of Wales, with a population of just 4,000 people, lost its biggest employer. It lost part of its identity. And, it lost a big chunk of its confidence.

In 2012, my wife Clare and I launched a denim brand called Hiut Denim Co. in order to get 400 people their jobs back. On the morning of 12 February our website went live. And boom. The orders started arriving.

And the orders kept on coming. It was exciting. A huge relief. And incredibly humbling. But we had received six months' worth of orders in the first month.

It was a nice problem to have, but a factory can't suddenly double its production. We had some stuff to work out. (Brace yourself: dumb decision alert.)

We made the decision to close the website. We stopped taking orders while we went away and doubled our staff. I know what you are thinking. But at the time, it seemed like the smart thing to do.

Our customers were just incredible. Some had to wait six months for a pair of jeans. But we knuckled down, worked super-hard, and finally, after months of late nights, we caught up on all our orders.

It was a great feeling. A big moment for us as a company and as a team. Thank you, Grandmasters. (That is what we call our machinists in the denim factory.)

Then we turned our website back on.

And boom. Nothing. No orders arrived. The world had forgotten about us.

To make matters worse, I had spent all our marketing budget on a coffee machine, doubled our staffing levels, and all our customers had got their jeans now so they didn't need any more.

We were on the very edge. Looking down.

It was at that precise moment that I got serious about our newsletter.

From that hyper-stressful day, everything we did, everything we built, every single piece of communication was geared towards building our community through our newsletter. And, oh boy, over the last four years we have learned how to do a newsletter well.

I love Instagram. I love Twitter. I love Medium. I have even begun to love Facebook. But without a newsletter, I couldn't gather all those people in one place and have a slower conversation with them.

Our newsletter is, without a doubt, our most critical tool for growing our business. Bar none. From that moment, when I chose a simple newsletter as the tool to tell the world we exist, it saved us. And now it is growing our business and helping us thrive. Phew. They say crisis makes a good editor.

So, yeah, I love newsletters. I want to share what we have learned with you to help you grow your business.

ACCORDING TO A 2014 STUDY BY MCKINSEY, FOR EVERY DOLLAR YOU PUT INTO EMAIL MARKETING YOU GET BACK 40× MORE THAN YOU WOULD THROUGH FACEBOOK, INSTAGRAM AND ALMOST EVERY OTHER MARKETING CHANNEL

CHAPTER ONE
TIME

YOUR BIGGEST COMPETITION IS THIS: PEOPLE ARE BUSY

When was the last time that you watched a film without looking at your phone? Or a football game? Or had dinner with your family? How many people have you seen driving while looking at their phone? How many people have looked at their phone while on the toilet? Be honest now.

And when we're not busy, we are finding lots of ways to help us forget how busy we are. Yoga is mainstream. Meditation, commonplace. Adult colouring books sell in the millions. We draw to forget. We look at a screen before we look at the sky.

Everything, everyone, wants our attention. And the one constraint is that we have the same amount of time we've always had before all these distractions came along. So understand this: Your newsletter has to stand out in a busy world when it drops into my inbox. Because I am busy.

WE ARE MORE
CONNECTED.
BUT LESS
PRESENT.

ATTENTION IS CHANGING

How we consume information today is changing. And it will continue to do so. What worked last year may suddenly stop working. Think about how we consume a TV show we love: we often binge-watch the whole series. We decide how and when we consume now, so in terms of a simple newsletter you have to fight for the right to have your subscribers' attention.

One way to try and carve a place in their busy week is to be consistent on the time: 11.30 a.m. every Sunday; or late on Thursday evening. You decide. But to create a habit, you have to be consistent.

WE NOW CONSUME IN MICRO MOMENTS

We set aside moments in the day to catch up on things. That may be on the commute to work. That may be at breakfast. That may be when the kids have just gone to bed. We look at things on the go, we look at things in between other things, we dual-screen and sometimes triple-screen. What we don't do is dedicate huge chunks of time to social media.

So if we are consuming in that hyper-speed way, we need to communicate with that in mind. We need to story-tell in lightweight and quick ways. That isn't to say long form doesn't work, and isn't brilliant, but there will be times when it absolutely won't cut through. Mostly when we can't give it our attention. We may have to break our communications down into easy-to-cope with bite-sized chunks.

The key thing here is to understand where the customer is in terms of their day, and tailor your newsletter accordingly. If they are commuting, it may need to be in a bite-sized form. Or if it's on Sunday, with a glass of wine, you can have more time with them.

WE CHECK OUR SMARTPHONE 221 TIMES A DAY. AND THEN WONDER WHY THE BATTERY GOES SO QUICK.

HOW TO RESPECT PEOPLE'S TIME? BE EXCELLENT

If you respect people's time – and I don't just mean by saying you do, but you actually do – then you will think hard before you send them a newsletter. You will do your best to make it super-useful. To make it truly inspiring. To make it deeply relevant. To make it as simple as you can. As beautiful as you can.

The amount of sheer effort you put into it shows respect for your customers' busy life by not adding to the dross they get sent each day. You won't have to tell them how much work goes into it, because they will be able to sense it, to feel it, to see it for themselves.

They will, by your actions, be able to tell that you respect them by only sending something worthy of their most precious asset: time.

DEEP WORK HELPS GET MORE DONE

In order for you to do newsletters well and give you amazing results, you have to invest time into making them great. Your team are already busy, so where will that time come from? Well, by training them in the art of deep work.

This is done by switching the distractions off. We live in a world with more distractions than ever. The smartphone is the ultimate attention-seeker.

To do their best work, your team will have to commit all their attention to it. And to do so for long periods of uninterrupted time. They will have to become ruthless at blocking out distractions.

Cal Newport has written a great book called *Deep Work*. In essence, you need to find two to three hours each day without wi-fi, without your phone, and make that part of your daily routine.

That two to three hours will be worth more than other people's eight hours. They may be working longer but they will be doing shallow work. They will be distracted by gossip in the open-plan office, by an email that has just arrived, by a great photo on Instagram.

When you are doing shallow work, you can't solve difficult problems. Your best work will require you to overcome difficulty. Your best work will stretch you, push you, find your very limits. This work cannot be done while thinking about something else.

For every distraction we get caught up in, it takes us another 20 minutes to get back into the flow of where we left. Distractions take more time than the distraction alone because they leave a residue, and it takes time to regain our focus.

Big companies have big teams. But they waste a lot of time, they have a lot of red tape, meetings that lead to another meeting but not to something happening fast. A small team can punch above its weight by not only being focused, but by focusing on the thing that will deliver the biggest results.

At Hiut Denim Co, we are an incredibly small team. We have organised our week in the following way by using the M+M method.

The first 'M' stands for Maintenance. These are the things you have to do to maintain your current position. And that takes most of your day. If you do that well, and it's vital that you do, you can hope to grow by at least 10 per cent.

The second 'M' is Momentum. The things that push you forward. The hardest thing about Momentum is finding the time to do it. You have to divide your day up so you make time for 'Momentum'. Momentum is the thing that will take you up to the next level. And beyond.

The culture you have to build in your company is to make everyone understand the importance of their day. And, how it has to be divided up to allow time for the things that will help you grow like crazy.

This photo is of Huw (Social Media Manager), who wanted to celebrate Leonardo Da Vinci's birthday. He thought it would give us Momentum. So he found time to buy some wood, and then build some wings with the help of Tim (our intern) one night.

He made a film and we shared it via our newsletter. It is one of the most viewed things we have ever done.

M+M
MAINTENANCE + MOMENTUM
= STRATEGIC USE OF TIME

IN ORDER TO DO YOUR BEST WORK, YOU WILL HAVE TO REPLACE DISTRACTIONS WITH FOCUS

WANT TO BUILD A NEWSLETTER THAT BUILDS YOUR COMPANY? THEN SPEND MORE TIME ON IT

Who knew? There is no single short cut that we can give you. But if you devote time and effort, work out your strategy that you think will make you stand out, then newsletters will work for you.

Of course, that will not suit everyone. There are those who want to find the easier path. But like most things, over time with continual effort and a smart strategy then it will work for you.

US studies have shown that for every $1 spent on a newsletter, there is a $40 return. Compare that to $7.30 for catalogues, or $17 for ad keywords. Plain and simple, newsletters are one of the best ways to grow a business. So spending time on it makes sense. And money.

CHAPTER TWO

STRATEGY

THE IMPORTANCE AND PSYCHOLOGY OF VALUE

The key to understanding how to win is to really understand the human being that you are going to send your newsletter to. Mostly, every newsletter they will receive this week will ask them to give or buy.

Rarely will a newsletter simply try and give them something useful, something inspirational, or an interesting bit of new information. And if it did, it would stand out.

Think of your newsletter as a relationship. A long-term one. The best relationships that last are those that both sides receive value from. In order to build a long-term newsletter, you will have to learn to give.

THE LAW OF RECIPROCITY

We are hard-wired to help people who help us. Social psychologists call it the 'Law of Reciprocity' – which is what makes humans want to give back, to help others, to return a good deed.

It is what makes humans so remarkable. It's important to understand this if you are going to adopt this as your strategy going forward. Not only does it feel like the right thing to do, but it will also help grow your business.

I think it is worth saying that you should do this because you believe in it, rather than just use it as another marketing strategy.

GIVING CREATES TRUST

We would do well to think of customer relationships as we would treat a friend. We would never have a friend that only ever asks for favours, only ever asks for something that would help them, only ever thinks of themselves. That is a one-way friendship, and tends not to last a lifetime.

I believe great companies give to their customers. And when they do there is a new connection between them which is called 'trust'. They did something for them that wasn't just about a transaction. Something that was given because it's good to do something without asking for anything in return. It means when you do finally ask your customer to buy from you, they think differently about you. It is not a short-term strategy, it is a long-term one. Relationships are best built over time – and on equal terms.

GIVE
GIVE
GIVE
ASK

No one likes a dinner guest who only talks about himself. And no one invites them back to their dinner parties. Sure, they're doing interesting things. Sure, they're amazing. Sure, the world needs to know they exist. But, jeez, they get boring. Quickly.

Likewise, most newsletters are boring us to tears. They sit down at the dinner table and just talk about themselves. It's kind of fun for a while. But just a short while. Then before you know it, you are looking at your watch and hoping some coffee is served to mark the end of the meal.

It doesn't have to be this way. Newsletters can be inspiring, useful and fun. But you have to do one thing: be interesting.

A great newsletter works by you sharing how you think about the world, and not just what you have to sell in this world. Remember, it's not all about you.

Gary Vaynerchuk understands this best. Read his books. Watch his talks.

THE PERSON AT THE DINNER PARTY WHO ONLY TALKS ABOUT HIMSELF NEVER GETS INVITED BACK

LESS DELIVERS MORE

Lots of companies think that sending more and more emails is the answer to growing their business. One key flaw to this strategy: the number one reason for unsubscribes is too much email marketing. And once they say goodbye, it is for good. Very few return.

So instead of the effort of doing many, how about doing fewer and making them mean more?

Excellence is a great business model. And if your newsletter suddenly becomes something that people look forward to, if your newsletter becomes useful, becomes inspiring, then the 'do less but better' strategy will pay off.

WHEN YOU ARE SELLING, SELL

A lot of companies will try and hide the fact they are selling with humour, or get to the point in a roundabout way. But the customer is intelligent, internet savvy and time-poor, so give them some respect. When you are selling, sell. Get to the point. 'Here's a great pair of jeans, please buy them. Here's a quick backstory. Would you like a pair?'

Don't leave them in any doubt that you are selling. They will make a decision if they want them or not. If they want them they will tell you by placing an order. If they don't want them they will tell you with the ultimate answer: silence.

Regardless of whether they want what you are selling or not at that moment, they will respect your directness.

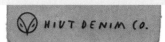

Do One Thing Well
June 2nd 2016
The 'Scrapbook Chronicles' will bookmark what
caught our eye, the stuff that inspired us, and log what
we are up to as a small denim company making our
way in this world. I hope you enjoy them.

The Tech Jean. More Sizes Now In Stock.
At 7.5oz, they're our lightest jean. They are designed
to give. Perfect for long-haul travel. Perfect for busy
days. And perfect for those long summer road trips.
Available in both Men's and Women's.

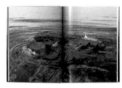

Dunn dunn. Dunn dunn. Dun dun, dun dun, dun...
Michael Muller has shot some of the most famous
faces in the world. But for his most recent book, he
ditched Hollywood and went into the wild to shoot
"the real celebrities." Sharks.

Scrapbook Chronicles

FACTORY TALK
HIUT DENIM CO.

CUTTING NEXT.

The Stolsby High Waist, one of our most popular women's jeans is going into production
next week. If we'd like us to make a pair in your size, make sure to order before Monday.

BUY

FREE REPAIRS.

Paul has been busy. He's been busy repairing. And busy learning his craft. I won't bore you
with the technicalities, but his repairs are now even better than before. But it takes him a
bit longer to do. If you are sending your jeans back for repair, there is currently a longer
wait. But as always, they are free repairs for life.

THE ROBOT LAWYER.

Factory Talk

USE DIFFERENT NEWSLETTERS TO DO DIFFERENT JOBS

We have two different newsletters: 'Scrapbook Chronicles' and 'Factory Talk'. One is very short. We use that to sell. And one takes time to read as it gives lots of food for thought. That one is giving.

'Factory Talk' covers only one thing. We use this to share our latest offer. 'Scrapbook Chronicles' has eight different categories. So it is quite long. In six of them we share pockets of inspiration. The remaining two categories top and tail the newsletter and are a chance for us to share what is happening in the company. They are not always selling something. More often they are sharing an update or some news.

MAKE ALL ROADS LEAD TO SIGN-UP

Think of Twitter as a road. Think of Facebook as a road. Think of Instagram as a road. They are fast-paced, busy roads. Blink for a second and the world whizzes by. That great post you put up a few hours ago? The world has moved on.

So what does that mean for your business? Well, one of the most important things you have to do is find a way to tell your story more on your own terms. Emailed newsletters allow for a longer conversation with your customer. And in a fast-paced social media world, that is pure and utter gold.

So one thing you should be thinking about is getting your Twitter, Facebook and Instagram followers to sign up to your newsletters. All roads should lead to newsletter sign-up. Because having a slower conversation in a crazy fast-paced world has become more important than ever.

OPTIMISE FOR LOYALTY

Once someone unsubscribes from your newsletter, that is them gone from your company forever. Forever is a long time. Ask a dinosaur. Once you understand that, you will think differently about sending a newsletter. The next time could be the last time if you don't get it right.

So, your job is to be the guardian of a long-term relationship. And the best way to have a long-term relationship is to stop thinking short-term. Think about how you build this relationship over a ten-year period.

Often we think we will get better results by doing more. But the opposite is true. The single biggest reason for people unsubscribing is mailing too often. Play the long game. Email less. Email better.

PERSISTENCE IS A SKILL

Everyone starts from zero. It's a tough place, but everyone begins there. But here's the thing: it takes time to build anything. And newsletters are no different. Many people start diets or exercise regimes and end up quitting. Likewise with newsletters. People start with good intentions, the right strategy, and they fizzle out. They don't see immediate transformation and so they adopt a sporadic schedule, or simply stop. I would view that as a good thing, because you are not going to do that. You know this will take time.

But you also know that if you continue to stick to the plan, then – over time, and not straight away – things will improve. So you carry on. Persistence is a quality some people are given.

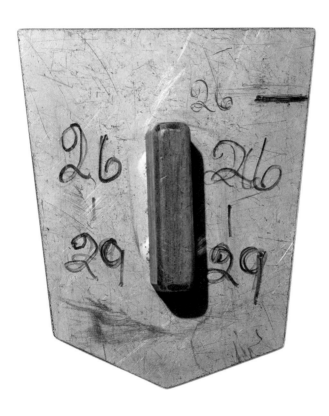

IT MATTERS

Let's start by saying this: design matters. If the design of your product matters to you, if the design of your website matters to you, if the design of your workspace matters to you, so should the design of your newsletter.

Here's why. Because your design can say things about your product or your service without having to resort to using words. It can say 'high quality', it can say 'fast service', it can say 'craft', just by the look and feel you choose. Say you have a community of 10,000 people and you email them four times a month. Over a three-year period, you would have sent out 1.44 million emails. Now is something that is going to be seen that many times worth the investment of time, money and consideration? I think so.

'THE DETAILS ARE NOT THE DETAILS. THEY MAKE THE DESIGN'

CHARLES EAMES

EVERYTHING SAYS SOMETHING

The typography will say something about you. The layout will say something about you. The photos you take will say something about you. Of course, your words will say something about you. But what do you want them to say? How do you want to position yourself: Fun? Serious? High quality? Innovative? All of the above?

Before you design anything, you should have a clear picture of your intent. Our design ethos at Hiut Denim Co is for understated, simple and well-made premium jeans. We use the design of our newsletter to back those values up.

What are your values? Write them down.

Before you ask a designer to look at your newsletter, make sure he or she gets it. Their design should sum up your values. So it works hard for you. Remember how many millions of times they are going to be sent out.

A good piece of design will evoke your values without needing to say them in words.

THE THINKING BEHIND THE HIUT DENIM CO

I realised how busy people were, so I wanted to make our newsletter feel like a place of calm. So spending five minutes at that place made them feel relaxed. We took inspiration from airports. Airports are designed to make you feel calm. Lots of people arrive stressed, late, anxious about flying. Mostly, airports are quite neutral for that reason. I took learning from that.

I briefed the design team to give it lots of white space, to pick photos with neutral backgrounds, and with words kept to a minimum. So they wouldn't overwhelm you. And, importantly, they would work well on smartphones.

We designed our newsletter so it was simple and uncluttered. We wanted to create a calm space for you to press the pause button. Where you can have a quiet five minutes by yourself to be inspired.

Calm also comes from the familiarity of regular features. And a consistent voice. In a world of information overload, less is indeed a very welcome thing. Our heads are so full of stuff; your newsletter should feel like an escape from a frantic, frenetic world. That way, people look forward to it.

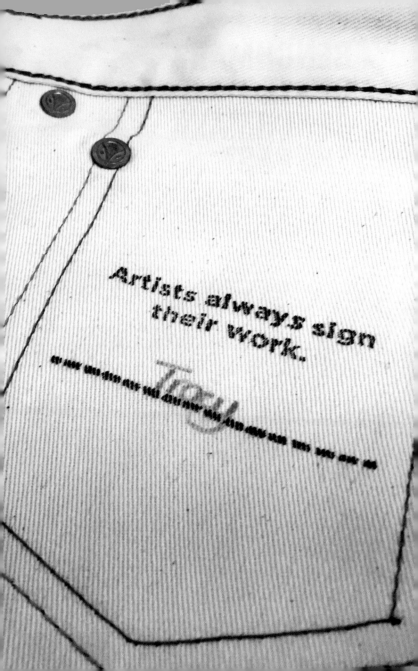

BENCHMARK OTHERS BUT BENCHMARK THE BEST

A good question to ask yourself is: What newsletters do I like? And an even better question is this: Why do I like them? What is it that has resonated with you? Then consider whether those attributes should find their way into your newsletter.

It is always good to benchmark a rival, but it is more useful to find someone who is pioneering new ways, even if it isn't your sector. Your sector may be dull, so if you just look at those who are doing it best, it may not push you as much as you need.

Here are some questions to ask about those who you benchmark:

— What is it they do well?

— What is the essence of what they are doing?

— How often do they send out a newsletter?

— How balanced is it? Give vs. Sell?

— Are they giving value?

— What could they improve on?

PICK YOUR ROLE MODELS CAREFULLY

Here are some examples of good newsletter design and what it is we like about them.

BEST MADE

bestmadeco.com

Based in New York, Best Made equip their customers with high-quality products empowering them to get outside, reconnect with their hands and nature, and in doing so 'embark on a life of great adventure'. Their newsletters have a clean and consistent design, good photography and they tend to give, as well as sell, something. They tell the story of the product and make it look good. They send newsletters quite frequently: we counted eight in August alone.

NEXTDRAFT

nextdraft.com

Again, coming out of the US, Dave Pell writes a funny social commentary on the news. He has a point of view that most newspapers simply couldn't get away with. No pictures, just short, pithy, ironic, brilliant text. The newsletter is sent about five times a week.

MONOCLE MINUTE

monocle.com/minute

Monocle's newsletter comes as a daily bulletin comprising five or six short stories around news, opinion and jobs illustrated with photographs. Content-wise, it's eclectic.

INSTAPAPER WEEKLY

instapaper.com

Instapaper's newsletter curates the seven top stories from the week with a focus on tech, design and business news.

KEVIN ROSE'S JOURNAL

kevinrose.com/newsletter

'A monthly newsletter for the curious', this one is always interesting and well curated. Good recommendations from a trusted source.

CUSTOMISE

We use MailChimp as our email sender. For us it is the simplest, the best, and it offers lots of templates that can get you started quickly. They have some big pluses. They are the turnkey – ready to go – and designed for sharing across other platforms like Facebook.

But when you code something yourself, it allows you to design something that exactly matches what you have in your head. This helps you to stand out. It shows that you care about design, that you have a great eye. And, it sets you apart from templates that anyone can use.

DESIGN A GREAT MASTHEAD

Every newspaper has a masthead. Every magazine does too. And so should your newsletter. It is the one thing that is a consistent element. It says your name. It says other things too if designed well. It can say you are serious, it can say you have a great sense of humour. It will appear in the same place, in the same size and the same positioning each week.

If you take a look at Dave Pell's masthead (*nextdraft.com*), it is iconic and, yes, it tells me the name, but it also gives me an idea that his viewpoint on the news is going to be, well, just a little bit more fun than everyone else's.

DESIGN FOR DEVICES

Mobile will soon become the number one place to see your newsletter. So as you sit at your computer designing your newsletter, and everything looks super-fine, do this. Send a test to your phone and see how it looks on the place most people will see it.

You will have to consider this more and more. Tools like MailChimp allow you to see this as you design it, so there is no reason to not get this right.

Also think about how it looks across different operating systems. Again, don't just look at yours. Look at how your customer sees it. And make sure it works.

'THE SIMPLER YOU CAN DESIGN SOMETHING THE MORE CLASSIC IT WILL BECOME'

PAUL ARDEN

CHAPTER FOUR

COMMUNITY

BUILD A COMMUNITY NOT A LIST

I would hope you want to build a community. A community is actively engaged. A community will tell you when you get it wrong. And when you get it right. A community will make suggestions, will give you ideas, and will share with other people on your behalf.

How do you build a community? The best way is to make them feel something for what you do. Reply to their comments. Have a dialogue. Have a conversation. Show you care. And they will show that they do too.

This is not a difficult thing. This is not rocket science. But you will only make time to do this if you care about your community. You can't fake it.

HOW DO YOU FIND YOUR COMMUNITY?

It's a good question. But it isn't a complex answer. Like attracts like. If you start talking about being a great cheese-maker, other people from the cheese community will find you. Yes, you can help that along a bit by telling the ten 'influencers' in your world that you are making great cheese. Hey, send them some. The mistake most people make is they want everyone to know what they are doing. But the truth is, the minority will inform the majority. There may be just a handful of influencers who you need to connect with. If they love what you are doing, they will tell their world. And then you are off.

Seth Godin has written a great book about community. It is called *Tribes*. And, I urge everyone to go out and buy it. It helped me understand community and how to go and find, connect and grow one.

A THOUSAND TRUE FANS

Kevin Kelly, the founding executive editor of *Wired* magazine, wrote a great piece about the music business. His theory was you only needed a thousand true fans to make a living from the music business. A true fan was someone who will buy almost everything you produce. From the limited edition 7-inch to the T-shirt to the mug to the tour tickets, etc. They blog about you, promote you, tell their friends about you. And the money they spend with you will allow you to make a living from your music. So, the importance of this theory is to know that you don't have to go broad to make your business work; instead you have to go narrow in order to mean a huge amount to a relatively small number of people. And build from there.

ENGAGEMENT
IMPORTANT

IS MORE
THAN SIZE

UNSUBSCRIBES ARE GOOD

Think differently on unsubscribes. No, you don't want to lose all your community. So yes, you will listen to unsubscribes. It will tell you information. It will tell you that you are becoming less relevant. You are emailing too often. You are not trying hard enough. But, because you have the greatest respect for your community's time, you don't want to waste their time with something they are no longer interested in; so you can change your mindset to celebrate when they leave.

And, of course, you will work even harder to keep the remaining community engaged by giving them value each and every time. If you can say you tried your hardest, cared the most, delivered more value than almost anyone else, then you can do no more than that.

PASSION = LEADERSHIP

A newsletter is more powerful when you show
leadership. And leadership comes from your passion.
Passion drives you to try harder, dig deeper, think
harder. Lots of people want to become a leader,
but they aren't willing to put in the work required.
Ultimately, you become a leader by showing and
demonstrating an unusual amount of love for what
you are doing. Your community can detect your
focus and effort, and when they feel it they are
willing to let you become their leader in this field.

DON'T DILUTE – BE NARROW

To build a strong and fiercely loyal community, you have to have a point of view. The mistake a lot of brands make is they want to be everyone's friend. And that makes the point of view, well, bland. The thing they want is a big following, and so they try to appeal to everyone. Oddly, they never achieve that thing they crave. They don't become influential. They don't get talked about. It is better to mean a great deal to a smaller community than meaning next to nothing to a huge community.

IF PEOPLE AREN'T ENGAGED, YOU KNOW WHO TO BLAME?

The law of interesting is simple enough.

Do interesting things and interesting things happen. That rule can be applied to newsletters too. So if your audience are not interested in what you are doing, it's kinda your fault.

It's because you haven't connected. It's because you haven't dug deep enough. It's because you haven't put new ideas across. It's because you are not doing it in a new way. It's because you have not thought about your story enough.

So rather than blame your tribe, ask yourself a difficult question: Why am I making this interesting subject so mind-numbingly dull?

A COMMUNITY WANTS CONNECTIONS, MEANING AND CHANGE

Understand what your tribe wants from you. And understand this: never in the history of the planet has there been a better time to connect people, provide meaning and help them change. Truly, the internet allows you to do this like never before. So before you set off, just work out how you are going to provide the connections and meaning and change for your tribe.

The more you can think about this before you start, the more likely you will be to connect from the start. The better you connect, the more it will grow.

Yup, it is better to do the hard thinking before you set off.

CHAPTER FIVE
CURATE

THE JOB OF THE EDITOR IS TO EDIT

This is one busy world. Attention is what you are after. But time is what no one seems to have. If you want people to spend time, their precious limited time, reading your darn newsletter, it'd better be good. Find new things. Find old things. Find amazing things. Put the hours in. Get known for finding great like-minded stuff. As their trusted editor, it is your job to find 'the gold'. So they don't have to.

INFORMATION OVERLOAD IS REDUCED BY GREAT CURATION. THE ROLE OF THE CURATOR HAS NEVER BEEN MORE IMPORTANT.

A SMALL TEAM IS A FAST TEAM

A supertanker kills the engine 20 minutes before docking, which is 15 miles. So you could say it takes 15 miles to stop. It's good to know that because we tend to spend a lot of time talking about how much bigger our rivals are than us. But if you view their size as their weakness, then you take a different view of your competition. And start to think how vulnerable they are to you, if you play to your strengths.

Their size makes them slow. And this world is speeding up. So play to your strength: that you are small. Small means fast. Small means responsive. You don't have to put your ideas to the board, you don't have to put them into research, you can put them into action instead.

The world is changing fast. And it will be those who are most nimble that will do the best. Don't be an ocean liner in a speedboat world.

THE RULES OF THE SPEEDBOAT

1. **SPEED IS MORE IMPORTANT THAN SIZE**
2. **DIRECTION CAN CHANGE QUICKLY – VALUES DO NOT**
3. **NO PASSENGERS**
4. **THE FEWER PEOPLE, THE QUICKER THE DECISIONS**
5. **YOU ARE HERE TO MAKE WAVES, NOT RIDE THEM**
6. **NO EGOS – THEY SLOW YOU DOWN**
7. **LISTEN TO YOUR GUT – THEN ACT**
8. **GOLIATH HAS HISTORY, BUT UP AHEAD IS THE FUTURE – GET THERE FIRST**
9. **THERE IS NO MAP – PIONEERS HAVE TO IMAGINE THE WAY, NOT READ IT**
10. **ALWAYS BE LAUNCHING**

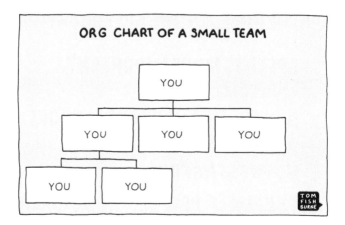

WHAT DOES A SMALL TEAM LOOK LIKE?

Well, if you looked in the mirror this morning, that would show you what a small team looks like. You have to wear many hats, huh? If you run a small business, as well as running the company and answering the phone, you are also the entire social media department. That includes the newsletter department too. In order to do all that, you have to be super-focused on your time. And learn to use the tools that you have at your hands to punch above your weight. Spend time learning how to use them – it will save you so much time. We've pulled together the ones we like to use on page 155.

AN EXAMPLE OF A SMALL TEAM

Hiut Denim Co. team members:

— **David:** Writer/Planner/Editor

— **Huw:** Curator/Builder/Optimiser

— **Paige:** Designer/Outreacher

The simple fact is we all find content throughout the week. We use the 'read laters' of Instapaper and Pocket to save all the bits we find throughout the week. Then during the content meeting we'll decide on what are the 'standouts'. Remember, if you share great stuff, your community will trust you and therefore your 'open' rates will be above average. Consistency builds your community. The moment you begin to let average content go out, then they trust you less.

CONTENT MEETINGS

HOW THEY WORK

Everyone should know their role. But everyone has to contribute towards finding and creating great content. A five-person team with only one person finding content is not as strong as a three-person team all on the hunt for great stuff. Law of averages. Also, law of diversity.

The vibe you want to create is important. At Hiut Denim we try to make sure great coffee is involved, in a great setting, and the meeting is light-hearted. It is competitive just because you want to find the best stuff, which is a good thing.

Everyone will know the stats from last week. And the activity this week. It is a very focused, very fast meeting. But fun.

OUR CONTENT MEETING

It happens each Monday morning. It lasts for an hour. It is perhaps the most important meeting of the week. Everyone contributes. By the end of the meeting we have agreed the content and strategy for our next campaign.

Purpose of Meeting
1. What worked
2. What didn't work
3. What are the stats? Sign-ups / Unsubscribes
4. Plan this week
5. What to share / what to create
6. Schedule timings
7. End of meeting – Go build

Agree Next Steps
1. Campaign activity
2. Write / Assemble / Preview
3. Schedule
4. Sign off
5. Send

EVERY COMPANY IS A MEDIA COMPANY NOW

INSIDE THE MIND OF YOUR AUDIENCE
MY HUSBAND
MY KIDS
MOM & DAD
CAREER
FRIENDS
WIFI
ME
TRAVEL
SUNSETS
HOME
I DON'T SEE OUR BRAND OF PICKLE RELISH ANYWHERE.
TOM FISHBURNE

VIEW YOUR CUSTOMER IN 360 DEGREES

Most companies only look at the world through their lens. If they make cheese, they talk only about cheese. But it's insightful for you to understand that your product is only a small part of your customers' interests. Be eclectic. Because your customers certainly are.

Your customer has other interests. They are not just about one thing. Nor are you. For example, you run a global sports brand. How do you separate music from sport? People listen to it when they run. They listen to it on the way to play a football match. The crowd sing songs to their team.

The human has a bunch of other interests apart from what you're trying to sell them. Do you ignore them? Do you want to see the whole human? Or just the part of the human that is relevant to you. Some say, just talk to them about your thing. I think a much more engaging way is to see the whole human. That is a better relationship.

INFLUENCERS' GO TO'S

Each week you will be finding or creating new content. In terms of finding great content, you have to be smart about it. Ask yourself the question: Who is always sharing or creating great stuff? Then follow them, bookmark them. You don't have to be looking at everybody. But you need to be watching your chosen sites like a hawk.

So set up an influencers list on Twitter or a bookmark list on your computer. It will be dependent on your needs but it will help you find great content with speed and regularity. So picking your influencers matters. They are your source. You will only be as good as they are.

Sometimes they stop producing, stop writing, or are just on holiday. Like a river, sometimes the source suddenly dries up. So you need to keep this list fresh with new people. But not too many. The whole thing with Twitter is that everyone follows too many accounts, so no one can keep up. The influencers list should be short, but great.

CHOOSE WHAT WORKS FOR YOU

Here are a few that we like:

- Flipboard
- Verge
- New York Times
- Product Hunt
- Mashable
- Uncrate
- Short of the Week
- Feedly
- Stumble Upon

- Brain Pickings
- Science Daily
- Outside Online
- Huffington Post
- Life Hacker
- It's Nice That
- Complex
- Cool Hunting
- Psychologies Magazine

Remember, if you look in the same place as everybody else, you'll share the same content as everyone else.

MAGAZINES

Subscribe to a new one a month. But find magazines which are not just the mainstream usual suspects. This will depend on your interests, but take time to flick through them. Make it a rule to tear something out of each one.

SCRAPBOOKS

Whether they are the real-life scrapbooks or Evernote digital ones, you will need to develop a system to keep all this content you find, and keep it somewhere where it can be accessed for when the time is right.

CREATE A TWITTER INFLUENCERS LIST

You can create a list on Twitter. A list is a curated group of Twitter accounts. You can create your own lists or subscribe to lists created by others. Viewing a list timeline will show you a stream of tweets from only the accounts on that list.

My advice – keep your influencers to fewer than 20. Pick a variety, but choose them well. They will determine how much you keep up to date. How much gold you find. This will become your Go To in terms of finding what is going on. Finding great stuff can be easy. Just get this organised.

To create a list on Twitter for iOS
1. From the Me tab, tap the gear icon.
2. Select View lists.
3. Tap the plus icon to create a new list.
4. Select a name for your list, and a short description of the list. The default setting for your list is public (anyone can subscribe to the list). To make the list only accessible to you, slide the switch next to Private to On.
5. Tap Save.

It isn't as easy to do on other platforms – Instagram, for example. But there are apps that will help you do it.

'I BEGAN TO REALISE HOW IMPORTANT IT WAS TO BE AN ENTHUSIAST IN LIFE. HE TAUGHT ME THAT IF YOU ARE INTERESTED IN SOMETHING, NO MATTER WHAT IT IS, GO AT IT AT FULL SPEED AHEAD. EMBRACE IT WITH BOTH ARMS, HUG IT, LOVE IT AND ABOVE ALL BECOME PASSIONATE ABOUT IT. LUKEWARM IS NO GOOD. HOT IS NO GOOD EITHER. WHITE-HOT AND PASSIONATE IS THE ONLY THING TO BE'

ROALD DAHL, MY UNCLE OSWALD

SHARING VS CREATING

Creating content takes time. Creating great content takes even longer. As a small team, you will be time-poor and time-stretched. It will be easier for you to find great content to share. Other people will have invested their time into making it, so you don't have to.

Sharing other people's great content makes a lot of sense when growing your newsletter list to a certain level. But to go to the next level, you will have to find the time to create your own content. Remember, it's the Momentum, rather than Maintenance, part of your day (see page 24). The thing that will push you forwards. Original content, assuming it's good, will get you more growth than just sharing other people's. That is because yours is unique. It's you.

HOW TO STAY INTERESTING

You need to keep your newsletter interesting to stay relevant. To hold your community's attention. That is why you need to understand the importance of the law of interesting.

Interesting things happen when you do interesting things. It's an equation, an unwritten law, and a universal truth all rolled into one. It's a way of looking at each day, at each opportunity, each time you meet someone.

It allows you to adopt a different viewpoint to failure, it invites you to trust in putting your work out there into the big wide world, and it gives you the freedom to be braver with your ideas, your work, and your thinking.

Interesting can help you. It can make your work better. It can open doors that you thought would never be open to you. It can help you work with amazing people and do amazing things.

Yes, interesting things happen when you do interesting things.

CHAPTER SIX

GROWTH

THE SIZE OF THE TRIBE DOESN'T MATTER. THEIR PASSION DOES.

EVERYONE STARTS FROM ZERO

Sucks, right? But everyone has to start here. So don't be embarrassed. The important thing is to start. Start with your outcome in mind. If your desire is to inspire the hell out of your community, work hard on their behalf. Sweat it. Dig deeper. Show them how much you care. If you can do that, and be consistent with your inspiration and usefulness, you will not stay small for long.

GROW ENGAGEMENT, NOT SIZE

Many companies like to tell you how big their list is. The numbers can be impressive. But let's not kid ourselves here. The key metric is engagement. It is the only number that counts. Engagement is the thing. The main thing. The only thing. Do I still open your newsletter? Because if I don't open it, what exactly are you boasting about? The fact that I and a million other people don't open your newsletter because it is no longer relevant to my life? That you have done such a great job of overselling to me? That if I could remember to unsubscribe to your newsletter I would in a heartbeat?

So yeah, the open rate tells you everything. It is the pulse. It is the vital signs. It tells you people are interested. Or not. It tells you everything you need to know. It tells you that you have done a great job. Or not. The size of the list doesn't tell you the truth. Engagement does.

'A SMALL LIST
THAT WANTS
EXACTLY WHAT
YOU'RE OFFERING
IS BETTER THAN
A BIGGER LIST
THAT ISN'T
COMMITTED'

RAMSAY LEIMENSTOLL

USE AN OPT-IN. THEY WORK LIKE CRAZY GOOD

Every day more people visit your website than you have in your newsletter community. That is an opportunity. These people have shown an interest in what you do, what you make. They may even be fans of everything you do.

Now here's a caveat. I used to think those pop-up 'Opt In' things sucked. But I have to concede they work. (See the graph opposite. The bit where we start growing a lot is where we introduce them.) The only thing I asked the team was, 'Can we do them well?' Not too spammy, not too desperate. And this is important: we start the relationship by giving. So give them something of value. At Hiut, we give them a free PDF of our YearBook.

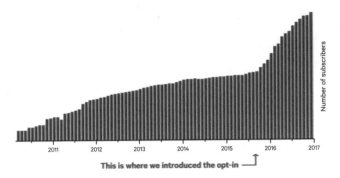

Hiut Denim Newsletter Subscriptions 2010–2017

Number of subscribers

2011 2012 2013 2014 2015 2016 2017

This is where we introduced the opt-in ⎯

YOU CAN SET THE POP-UP SO IT'S A GOOD FIT WITH YOUR BRAND

If you know how long the average person stays on any of your pages, you can create a timed pop-up to capture their address. For example, if visitors usually stay eight seconds on our page, the pop-up timer should be set to five seconds to guarantee the maximum amount of impressions possible.

Sumo is a great tool to execute this type of pop-up. If you know only 20 per cent of readers get to the bottom of your page, you can create a pop-up that appears at a certain section of your page.

You can set a sign-up through your product pages too. And when you send them a receipt. It's up to you what feels right for your brand.

OWN A TIME

Create a habit. Send your newsletter out at a specific time. And keep to it. We like routine. We like regular. What we don't like are surprises (Christmas and birthdays aside). That is why it's good for your newsletter to create a regular timeframe. You know, like the Instapaper weekly. The Monocle Minute. Swiss Miss's Friday Link Pack. So even if we are super-busy, and we get one of these emails through, we don't get annoyed. We know it. It always comes at that time. This week, I am just too busy to read it. But hey, I will be less busy next week. And will catch up with it then.

WE FINALLY FOUND A WAY TO GET PEOPLE TO ENGAGE WITH OUR CONTENT.

PEOPLE SHARE GREAT OR NOT AT ALL

People don't share average. People don't share what they have already seen. Nor do they share the meh, the so-so, the lame. They share useful, inspiring and, yes, the slightly dumb at times.

The word remarkable came from people remarking upon something. They did so because it stood out. It was memorable. It caught their attention. If you want to adopt a strategy for growth, try embarking on a strategy for the remarkable. People will do the work for you. They will do the heavy lifting. They will do the best thing for growth – tell their friends on your behalf.

COMPETITIONS ARE CRACK

People love competitions. They work. They certainly build your community quickly. And, if done with some skill, they can build a great community. But you have to be careful not to build a community that has come to you just because it had the chance of winning, in our case, one of the world's finest pair of jeans.

Even though they discover you through a competition, you want to design it so there are shared values and interest. Then you can start to have a conversation over time with them, and one day they may buy a pair of jeans.

12 TOOLS
FOR GROWTH

1. **SIGN-UP PAGE**
2. **OPT-IN POP-UP**
3. **WELCOME EMAIL**
4. **COMPETITIONS**
5. **WRITE BLOGS**
6. **TWITTER CARDS**
7. **GUEST POSTS**
8. **FORWARD TO A FRIEND**
9. **PR**
10. **CREATE CONTENT**
11. **LEARN TO WRITE HOOKS**
12. **OFFLINE EVENTS**

TWO SINS:

MAILING TOO OFTEN MAILING TOO LITTLE

What's the answer? I know for our community, it's around four times a month. But, that may be different for you. It may be once a week. It may be once a day. You will have to find out for yourself.

It's a great tool. Use it sparingly. The unsubscribe button will tell you if you have got it wrong. But don't underuse it, either. Social media is brutal. People forget you pretty damn quick. It's nothing personal; everyone is just plain busy. So how often should I send a newsletter? Well, that's a tough one. You will just have to find the right balance. Mind you, like your car keys, that isn't always the easiest thing to find.

PEOPLE REMEMBER REMARKABLE. THEY FORGET THE MUNDANE

If you invest in building a remarkable newsletter, it will pay off. You can measure it. You can count every click. You see the response rate. This will not be a case of 'I think it is working'. You will know. Newsletters are binary. Zero tells you it didn't work. One is that it worked.

Yes, it will take time to build your community. No, there aren't many short cuts for that. Yes, if you want to build it well, it means you can't always be selling. But embrace the counter-intuitive. When you give, and keep giving, it will come back to you.

FINDING YOUR VOICE

The thing that binds us all together is that we're human. But when we start to write a newsletter we often forget that. We forget we have a great sense of humour. We forget our vulnerabilities. We forget the very things that make us damn well human. Yes, humans swear. Who knew? All those things, warts and all, are the very things that make us weird but also make us interesting. And, at the end of the day, human. So don't write, 'To whom it may concern'. You're not that person. I want to hear you. I want to hear the human sitting behind the computer. I want to hear the human behind the company. I want to hear the human behind the not-for-profit. Let people in. Be human.

'HERE'S A SIMPLE TRICK TO GET MORE PEOPLE TO READ WHAT YOU WRITE: WRITE IN SPOKEN LANGUAGE'

PAUL GRAHAM, FOUNDER OF VIAWEB

WRITE LIKE YOU TALK

Sometimes you read things and think, 'What the hell does that mean?' Normally, it is by clever people, but they can't put things down on paper in a language that you and I can understand. But if they could talk about it, you'd get it. That happens a lot. Gobbledygook is not in short supply.

So, there's one way to avoid this – and it's annoyingly simple: just read what you have written out loud. You listening to what you have written is one of the best bullshit detectors around. It makes things clearer. It shows up complicated explanations. It helps with poor spelling, too. If you have the patience to do it, and can make it part of your editing process, it will help you sound more like, well, you.

HUMOUR = HUMAN

Want to know why people like GIFs so much? It's because they're funny. Irreverent. Stupid. Dumb. Addictive. And yeah, we can't get enough of them. The one thing that doesn't cost a ton of money is our sense of humour. It is one of our key defining attributes. And if you want people to connect with you and your newsletter, it is one of best currencies to connection that I know. People connect while laughing their heads off. Without saying it, it reminds people there is a human behind this thing. Not a committee, not a corporation, but a real human being with a pulse.

'YOU CANNOT BE A POWERFUL AND LIFE-CHANGING PRESENCE TO SOME PEOPLE WITHOUT BEING A JOKE OR AN EMBARRASSMENT TO OTHERS'

MARK MANSON, THE SUBTLE ART OF NOT GIVING A F*CK

VOICE IS MORE THAN JUST WORDS

It can be. How. You say it. It can be your punky attitude. Your irreverence. Your pithiness. Your long-form brilliance. But voice can take other forms than just words. It could be the photos you choose. The illustrations you pick. The colours you choose for your newsletters. It could be your sheer energy to do one a day. It could be your positivity. It could be the love of your subject. It could be your take on the world. It could be your sense of design. So think of voice in a 360 degrees kind of way. There are many ways to find your voice. Which one best expresses you and your brand/project/whatever?

BE YOU

No one else can be you. Be inspired by others, but don't follow them. Share things you are passionate about, not what you think will get the most likes. If it matters to you, then chances are it matters to others too. So share it. Let it come from you. When you write, make it feel like you are speaking. Warts and all. Developing your voice won't come in just one newsletter, but it will come over time. Be funny. Be emotional. Just don't be corporate. Not everything has to have a business reason. Write about what is on your mind, what is inspiring you. Where you are right now. You know the stuff only you could talk about. Only you can be you. It's the closest thing you will get to being a monopoly.

LISTEN TO YOUR GUT

Sometimes people overthink things. And when that happens, something is lost. Sometimes the first thing you write is the purest. When you go over it, you make it more polished. And, in lots of ways, it's better. But it is missing that little something. Sometimes we make things safer, we just don't want to stand out too much. But again, by doing that, we lose our point of view. We sanitise it. We take the bumps out. But, ask yourself this: What's your gut telling you? You have to learn to trust your instinct.

Here's something I wrote to help me find my voice when building my businesses. A lot of this can be applied to your newsletter.

10 STEPS TO FINDING YOUR VOICE

1. BE CLEAR

Define the purpose of your company. Do this alone. Do not consult anyone but yourself. One sentence should do it. Write it on a paper napkin and pin it to the wall. Once decided upon, you cannot change it. Make sure that you are excited by it. Make sure you are willing to spend the rest of your life working towards it. Make sure it is your real purpose and not just what other people want to hear. Make sure it lives in your head and, just as importantly, in your heart.

2. BE FOCUSED

Define your product and its purpose. And stick to it. Stop making product that is not consistent with your definition of where you sit in this world. Even if it makes money, stop making it. Narrow the focus. Google achieved more by offering less than its competitor. Rather than closing down opportunities, going narrower opens them up. Those who spend their days trying to be all things to all people rarely have time to change the world.

3. BE YOURSELF

Don't try to be like others. Don't follow or mimic.
Don't pretend. A voice doesn't come from a meeting
or a committee. Or from the latest trend or, for that
matter, the latest piece of research. It comes from
one person: the books they have read, conversations
shared, experiences endured. The voice is fragile
in the wrong hands. Be careful whom you give the
task to. The strength of Nike was that advertising
exec Dan Wieden got inside the head of founder
Phil Knight when he came up with 'Just do it'. He
understood that Knight was a super-competitive
sports nut who wanted to crush the competition.
And he kept relaying that to his customers. Year
after year. Come rain, come shine.

4. BE EMOTIONAL

You have to make your customers feel something.
Understand what is in their hearts. Logic is a blunt
tool in this regard, my friend. It makes perfect sense,
it ticks all the boxes, but it changes very little.
You need a different set of tools. Those tools will
comprise music, pictures and words that, when
shaken up and put back in the right order, will leave
your customers inspired. Oh, by the way, this is not
easy to do. Give them meaning by all means, but
don't give them ads. Bare your soul. Tell your
struggle. Tell your pain. Tell your lows. A corporation
finds it hard to show its soul as it rarely has one.
Be vulnerable. Be honest. But most of all, be you.

5. BE INSTINCTIVE

Research nothing. Listen to what you feel. If you are in doubt, ask your partner. If you are still in doubt, ask your kids. Go no further than the circle that you trust. Ever.

6. BE USEFUL

Make products for a purpose. That chase a function and not a fashion. Invent for your customers' needs. Small needs can become big business. If you suddenly become fashionable, it is because you have chased being useful. Customers can decode real from fake in the blink of an eye. If you try to be of a moment, you will die in the moment, once it has had its time. Instead, carry on making products that have a use. Be authentic. If you can say that, you are on solid ground. Don't get sidetracked by chasing fashion.

7. BE THE CHANGE

To support your purpose, you need more than just words. You have to change your industry; you have to show another way. And you have to communicate that change in the most inspiring way that a human can imagine. Look at how well Apple communicates change. Every revolution needs an enemy. Challenge design, challenge pollution, challenge landfill, challenge people's 'buy and throw' culture. Now that you can make anything, what does your company want to make? And, even more than that, what does it want to change?

8. **BE CONSISTENT**

A great business is built over time. A company's product, its purpose and how it speaks to the world needs to be consistent. Stay true. The financial world fully understands the concept of compound interest and how a small change can make a big difference. Similarly, a small compromise here and there, can accumulate over time to change the very soul of a business. The rule of consistent product and service is easy to understand. But the same rule needs to be applied to a company's voice.

9. **BE RELEVANT**

Understand your customer. And make product that is relevant to their lives. Remember, the worst thing you can do for the environment is to make something that no one wants to buy. Speak to them in a way that connects with them and makes them feel something. The trick to this is to give something of yourself. If you feel something, the chances are so will they. This is not rocket science. It's just gut instinct. It's knowing what they are into because you are into it too.

10. **BE POSITIVE**

A business needs to do the numbers, but it also needs a purpose. That gives you the passion. Humans need that. So use your business to go and make a positive change. Be the hope. Hope is a rare, quietly powerful thing. Remember, the cynic changes little or nothing. The optimist can and will. Spread wonder. Spread optimism. It's the best stuff.

CHAPTER EIGHT

HOOKS

'ON THE AVERAGE,
FIVE TIMES AS MANY
PEOPLE READ THE
HEADLINE AS READ
THE BODY COPY.
WHEN YOU HAVE
WRITTEN YOUR
HEADLINE, YOU HAVE
SPENT EIGHTY CENTS
OUT OF YOUR DOLLAR'

DAVID OGILVY

WHAT IS A HOOK?

A hook is another word for a headline. And for
newsletters, your headline is the subject line.
The word hook has more meaning in the digital world.
It is written to get you to click. It must have enough
self-interest – in this time-poor world – for you to
want to find out more by clicking on it. It needs to pull
you in, to give you a promise, to ask a question that
you want answered, to make you curious, to give you
some urgency for doing so. So yes, there is an art to it.

WHY SUBJECT LINES MATTER MORE THAN EVER

Here's the deal. You research your newsletter.
You compile it. You select the illustrations or photos.
You write some great words for hours. Then you
check the links, the spelling. And when you are
finally happy, it's good to go. And then, get this,
you give a minute's thought to the subject line.
You know, just before it goes out. So the thing that
is the biggest factor of all for people opening it gets
a single minute or two of your attention. Now, look
at it like this. This thing that is the single determiner
of its success should get the most time. Not just a
minute before you press send.

HOW BUZZFEED LOOKS AT A HEADLINE

BuzzFeed almost invented the word clickbait. They take their headlines very seriously. They don't leave them to the last minute. They understand that if the headline doesn't get clicked, then the story doesn't get read. So what do they do? Well, they have a culture of testing to find out what headline is going to work. So they write around 25 headlines per article to make sure they find the most viral one. The headlines get their attention, because that is what decides the failure or success of their articles.

'FOR SALE: BABY SHOES, NEVER WORN'

FAMOUS SIX-WORD SHORT STORY,
ATTRIBUTED TO ERNEST HEMINGWAY

EMOTIONAL HEADLINES PULL BEST OF ALL

Dr Hakim Chishti studied the roots of several languages including Persian, Aramaic, Hebrew, Arabic and Urdu. From doing this he discovered the importance of Emotional Marketing Value (EMV).

His research found that there are basic underlying harmonics in language that are always interpreted with the same 'emotional' reactions. Where dictionary-based meanings can be mistaken, the sound tones themselves are always interpreted the same way in our emotional response. This means that emotional language creates a very predictable response, something that can be very advantageous to marketers.

THE HIGHER THE EMV SCORE, THE MORE SHARES

The Emotional Marketing Value (EMV) is a score that looks to assess how a group of words follow these emotional harmonics, and how likely they are to elicit an emotional response from a reader.

The Emotional Marketing Value Headline Analyzer (*aminstitute.com/headline*) is a tool based on the research that is made freely available by the Advanced Marketing Institute.

Most professional copywriters' headlines will have 30 to 40 per cent EMV words in their headlines, while the most gifted copywriters will have 50 to 75 per cent EMV words in headlines. It may sound uber-geeky, but it works. The good thing is you can put your headlines through the AMI tool for free.

One important insight is that positive, upbeat headlines draw a much more positive response and are much more likely to be shared. Hell, yes. Let's be positive.

THREE EMOTIONAL TYPES

1. ## FACTUAL
   Words that are especially effective when offering products and services that require reasoning for careful evaluation.

2. ## EMPATHETIC
   Words that bring out strong emotional reactions in people.

3. ## SPIRITUAL
   Words that have the strongest potential for influence and often appeal on a deep emotional level.

IT IS SPRING.

AND I AM BLIND.

AN EXAMPLE OF EMV

This may or may not be a true story. I am not sure. But it serves to make a point. An advertising copywriter saw a blind man in Regent's Park with a sign that read: 'I am blind. Please give.' To help him raise more money, he rewrote the sign to read: 'It is spring. And I am blind.' That made the passers-by think about what it must be like to not see all the beautiful flowers, the trees turning green, the birds making their nests. It made them empathise with the blind person. And once that happened, they gave more money.

UNDERSTAND THE PSYCHOLOGY

Why do people share on social media? Well, it is a complex answer because it involves understanding why a human does something. Good luck with that. But a fascinating study was conducted by the *New York Times* Customer Insight Group. This study found that people share things for five common reasons:

— To reveal valuable and entertaining content to others

— To define themselves to others

— To grow and nourish relationships

— For self-fulfilment

— To help spread the word about brands and causes they like or support

In other words, people share content because they value the people they surround themselves with and either want to elevate their own status or help friends and peers improve their own lives.

WHAT GIVES A SUBJECT LINE HOOKINESS?

1. It makes an emotional promise.

2. It creates a curiosity gap. A need to know that drives people to click.

3. It is relevant to the desired customer. Uses words that your people relate to.

4. It appeals to the readers' self-interests. Tell them the benefit.

5. They want to know who is speaking to them. Include the brand name.

6. A longer headline with meaning will beat a shorter one with none.

7. Be positive. We prefer sunshine and rainbows to doom and gloom.

8. The headline should not be blind. It should be understood on its own.

9. Ask a question that makes it compelling to know the answer.

10. How-To's? Oh, boy, do we love to learn. And, we love an infographic too.

11. Give the headline some urgency. Limited time-frame. Offer ends soon. FOMO is real.

12. Understand the psychology of where your readers are at that moment, in their lives.

13. And yeah, lastly, we love lists.

CHAPTER NINE

TEST
TEST
TEST

MEASURE IT IMPROVE IT

There is almost nothing you can't test on a newsletter. You can test which day of the week is best for your community. You can test the time of day – morning, afternoon or evening.

Should your newsletters be shorter? Or longer? More frequent maybe? Once a week? Once a month? Should it have more photos? More illustrations? Would it work better if it was funnier? Or should it be more serious? Plain text vs HTML? Emotive subject lines? Should your subject lines ask a compelling question?

If you can think of something to test, there will be a way to test it. And, over time, you can build up a pretty clear picture of what makes your community tick.

'TAKE NOTHING ON ITS LOOKS; TAKE EVERYTHING ON EVIDENCE. THERE'S NO BETTER RULE'

CHARLES DICKENS, GREAT EXPECTATIONS

HEADLINES... YOU KNOW WHAT TO TEST THE MOST

I have spoken earlier about the importance of the headline (the subject line for a newsletter). Even after doing all that work on your headline, you can still test it further. You can do an A/B test. This is basically an 'either/or' test. You simply test which one is clicked the most (you can set the criteria). This test goes out to a small portion of your newsletter community, and after four hours (or whatever time period you choose) there will be a winner. And then, your whole community will be sent the winning subject line that has shown the most engagement.

According to MailChimp, 28 to 39 characters for a subject line was the 'sweet spot' with the highest click rate in a study of 200 million emails. That is about ten words. Ten vital words. Ten words that can grow your business.

A/B TEST EVERYTHING

You can A/B test pretty much anything:

— What day of the week gets better open rates?

— Does a subject line with an incentive or a teaser work best?

— Does including your company name in your subject line increase engagement?

— Is it better to use your name as the 'from' name, or your company name?

— Does the time of day a campaign is sent affect the click rate?

— Are subscribers more likely to click a linked image or linked text?

— Do subscribers prefer a campaign that contains a GIF or one with static images?

TEST INTERESTS

Even in a small company like Hiut Denim Co, some customers are solely focused on one product. They may love Japanese Selvedge denim, so an email from us selling a Tech Jean will not sit well. So, respect their time by taking the trouble to not send them something you are pretty sure won't be of interest to them. Even better, when you sign them up, try and find out what emails *will* be of interest to them. That way, you can put a filter in early on and will have saved on testing the segmentation of your community. But, if you haven't, then test you must.

TEST LANDING PAGE

As a company grows, they may send multiple newsletters to different segments of their community. For example a runner who clicks on to Patagonia may want to subscribe to a running newsletter and not a general one. At this stage, your website won't be able to welcome each segment with a relevant message. That is why you will have to build a landing page for a specific campaign or side of your business. Well, you can A/B test these too. You can find out which layout works best, which words resonate, which photos pull people in, which design makes them want to find out more. Yes, all this testing takes time. But you are here to build your business, and these little tweaks can – and do – make a difference. I know, I know – no short cuts here, either. Damn.

'WHAT GETS MEASURED, GETS MANAGED'

WILLIAM THOMSON, LORD KELVIN

TEST ONE THING AT A TIME

A while back I was asked to write the brand book for Dyson Ltd. I wanted to meet James Dyson so I said yes. Even today, the thing that I still marvel at is that he spent four years doing one iteration at a time. In total, he did 5,127 iterations to make his vacuum cleaner work. I don't know anyone who has his level of sheer determination to make something work. He deserves every bit of the success he gets. So, I am not saying you have to spend four years in a shed trying to work this out. But, I am saying test one thing at a time. Otherwise, you are going to get yourself in a pickle. Make notes. And, slowly, build a picture up of what works best for you. What works for me will be different to what works for you. You can't borrow other people's results. You have to test your data with your people. Yup, no short cuts to be had here.

CHAPTER TEN

CHECKLIST RITUAL

DON'T SEND UNTIL?

Your newsletter should uphold your standards. There is a lot to get right. And it's easy to get even the simple things wrong. But as much as you are in a rush to send it out, before you do: Check. Double-check. Triple-check.

When you make a single mistake, depending on your list size, it will be seen by thousands, hundreds of thousands of times. Last week we sent out an email in which we spelt *Vogue* wrong. It happens. We missed that one. But mostly we catch them before they go global.

Having a checklist before you send something out is a must. It's a discipline that you should instil in your team.

CHECKLIST RITUAL

- ☐ **CHECK THE RIGHT TO USE PHOTOS**
- ☐ **LIST CLEANED**
- ☐ **PRINT OUT FOR READ THROUGH**
- ☐ **SPELL-CHECKED**
- ☐ **DEVICE-CHECKED**
- ☐ **EMAIL PROVIDER CHECK**
- ☐ **CHECK IT'S THE RIGHT LIST**
- ☐ **LINKS CHECKED**
- ☐ **LOADING SPEED CHECKED**
- ☐ **SUBJECT LINE CHECKED/TESTED**
- ☐ **TEST LINE SENT**
- ☐ **TEST SENT**
- ☐ **PRE-MORTEM***

* Ask why it may fail, rather than why it did fail

FOR ME THE NEWSLETTER IS THE MOST IMPORTANT TOOL THAT I HAVE IN BUILDING A GLOBAL DENIM BRAND. SECOND ONLY TO THE SEWING MACHINE.

It's always good to think of someone else's newsletter that you always read and ask yourself why you stick with it. There will be elements in it that really you should find in yours. You are trying to do something you like too. You should be your toughest audience.

For me the newsletter is the most important tool that I have in building a global denim brand. Second only to the sewing machine. Yes, you have to invest time, you have to put effort in, but more than anything you have to understand the methodology of what you are doing. When you do that – as I hope I have shown you here – you will see the results you set out to achieve. Good luck.

I will leave you with some things I've learned from producing lots of newsletters...

23 CRAZY SIMPLE TIPS ABOUT HOW TO BUILD A HIGH-GROWTH NEWSLETTER

1. Spend more time on it (who knew?)
2. Be like a train. Know where you are going
3. Your biggest competition is for people's time
4. View your customer in 360 degrees
5. Give value
6. Benchmark ... but benchmark from the best
7. Design matters
8. A small team is a fast team
9. Deep work helps you grow
10. Mobile, mobile, mobile
11. Optimise for loyalty
12. Creating beats sharing
13. Be the editor
14. Attention is changing
15. Test, test, test
16. Don't leave subject lines to the last minute
17. All roads lead to sign-up
18. Use and master the tools for an easy life
19. Engagement is more important than size
20. Everyone starts from zero
21. Consistency creates trust
22. Be human
23. Have a checklist ritual

'BUILDING AN EMAIL LIST IS THE SINGLE BEST WAY TO COMMUNICATE WITH YOUR AUDIENCE, PERIOD. BETTER THAN FACEBOOK, BETTER THAN TWITTER, BETTER THAN ADS. BECAUSE YOU OWN IT. BECAUSE IT IS A RELATIONSHIP OF MUTUAL TRUST AND OPT-INS. THAT IS WHY YOU NEED TO BUILD ONE'

RYAN HOLIDAY

RESOURCES

CURATE

Geeky resources to help you curate
There are tons of them out there. As time goes on, new ones will appear and some of these will go:

Feedly
Organise, read and share what matters to you.

Timeline JS
Create embeddable, responsive timelines. Using Google spreadsheets, this allows you to build rich timelines that include videos, photos and tweets.

SoundCloud
SoundCloud is a global online audio distribution platform. You can upload, record, promote and share original audio files.

Piktochart
Infographics are awesome tools for displaying data-driven content, but they're hard to create from scratch. Piktochart uses template and drag-and-drop tools to make the process much easier.

Infogr.am
Another tool for creating infographics, but this one works best with spreadsheets of data.

Storify
Storify allows users to curate tweets and other posts to create a story around news or an event then embed into your own site.

Thinglink
This is an easy way to make images interactive. Upload an image, tag it, then embed it on your site.

Wordle
Word clouds are a cool way to add context to a presentation. Visual elements like this make content infinitely more shareable.

Slideshare
An often overlooked tool for content marketing, this creates a deck and can draw attention to a resource or service on your website. One deck on YouTube drew 20k-plus views to the creator's content.

Polldaddy
Surveys and quizzes are another way to make content interactive and interesting. A good way to breathe new life into old posts.

Google Public Data Explorer
There is an insane amount of data here and Google has made it all very easy to navigate and share.

50 Content Marketing Tools
A good list from the kissmetrics blog.
blog.kissmetrics.com/50-content-marketing-tools

HOOKS

Tool for measuring the emotion of a headline
aminstitute.com/headline

TOOLS FOR AN EASY LIFE

Mailchimp
This is the service we use to send our newsletters out. It is super-simple and easy to use. It is free if you have below 2,500 people in your community. Around 14 million people use it.

Instapaper
Instapaper is the simplest way to save and store articles for reading later: offline, on-the-go, perfectly formatted. Just press the 'read later' button when browsing and your article is saved.

Pocket
Like Instapaper, this allows you to save interesting articles, videos and more for later. Once saved, the list of content is visible on any device – phone, tablet or computer.

Hootsuite
Hootsuite is a platform to help you manage your social media and plan activities. Your Hootsuite dashboard supports Twitter, Facebook, Instagram, Linkedin, Google+, YouTube and many more.

Twitter Polls
Twitter Polls allow you to weigh-in on questions posed by other people on Twitter. You can also easily create your own poll and see the results instantly.

Clear
Super-easy to use To Do list app. Swipe to the right to check an item off the list, swipe left to delete, and pull up to clear completed items. We use it on our phones to keep check of outstanding tasks.

Google Trends
A useful website resource that allows you to find out the latest trends, data and visualisation from Google. You can set up email alerts on particular subjects.

Trello and Basecamp
The ultimate project management tools. Both apps are a great way for a team to keep track of what needs doing, what has been done, and by whom.

Instagram
One of the most used platforms in the world, Instagram is a super-easy way to share photos of your products and activity with your community. Useful when compiling newsletters as it forms a visual diary.

Grammarly
A writing-enhancement platform, Grammarly's proofreading and plagiarism-detection resources check for a writer's adherence to more than 250 grammatical rules.

WeTransfer
WeTransfer is a cloud-based file-transfer service designed to send small and large files. You can send up to 2GB in the free version.

Dropbox
Dropbox is a file-hosting service that offers cloud storage, file synchronisation, personal cloud, and client software.

ABOUT THE AUTHOR

David Hieatt is not a theorist. He has built brands from nothing, with next to nothing, just by understanding a few basic rules. The 'Scrapbook Chronicles' newsletter has become a cult offering from his company, the Hiut Denim Co. Its open rate exceeds almost any industry standard and it's one of those rare newsletters that people actually look forward to receiving. Not only that, it has delivered results. It has grown the company by 25 per cent each year for the last three years. And each year for the last three years, the company has turned a profit. David is also the co-founder of the Do Lectures – an annual gathering around ideas – and has spoken at Apple, Google and Red Bull, amongst others. He is the author of *Do Purpose: Why brands with a purpose do better and matter more* (published 2014) and *The Path of a Doer* (2010, reissued 2020). He also runs workshops and online courses with the Do Lectures based on the ideas in *Do Purpose* and *Do Open*.

ABOUT THE CARTOONIST

Tom Fishburne started publishing his cartoons with a simple weekly email newsletter in 2002, while working in marketing. His cartoons are now read by hundreds of thousands of marketeers each week. In 2008, Tom attended the very first Do Lectures event and was inspired to figure out how to turn his cartooning hobby into a livelihood. In 2010, he left his marketing job to start a business with his wife that helps tell marketing stories with cartoons. Their Marketoonist studio has grown to include several cartoonists and works with Google, LinkedIn, Kronos, and many other brands. In 2011, Tom returned to the Do Lectures, this time as a speaker. His weekly email newsletter is still the most important way Tom shares cartoons with his audience and grows the business. You can find Tom at: *marketoonist.com*

Books in the series

Do Agile Tim Drake
Do Beekeeping Orren Fox
Do Birth Caroline Flint
Do Breathe
    Michael Townsend Williams
Do Build Alan Moore
Do Death Amanda Blainey
Do Design Alan Moore
Do Disrupt Mark Shayler
Do Earth Tamsin Omond
Do Fly Gavin Strange
Do Grow Alice Holden
Do Improvise Robert Poynton
Do Inhabit Sue Fan, Danielle Quigley
Do Lead Les McKeown
Do Listen Bobette Buster
Do Make James Otter

Do Open David Hieatt
Do Pause Robert Poynton
Do Photo Andrew Paynter
Do Present Mark Shayler
Do Preserve
    Anja Dunk, Jen Goss, Mimi Beaven
Do Protect Johnathan Rees
Do Purpose David Hieatt
Do Scale Les McKeown
Do Sea Salt
    Alison, David & Jess Lea-Wilson
Do Sing James Sills
Do Sourdough Andrew Whitley
Do Story Bobette Buster
Do Team Charlie Gladstone
Do Walk Libby DeLana
Do Wild Baking Tom Herbert

Also available

Path A short story about reciprocity Louisa Thomsen Brits
The Skimming Stone A short story about courage Dominic Wilcox
Stay Curious How we created a world class event in a cowshed Clare Hieatt
The Path of a Doer A simple tale of how to get things done David Hieatt

Available in print, digital and audio
formats from booksellers or via our
website: **thedobook.co**

To hear about events and forthcoming
titles, you can find us on social media
@dobookco, or subscribe to our newsletter